KEENE PUBLIC LIBRARY
60 Winter St.
Keene, NH 03431
352-0157

D1480674

KEENE PUBLIC LIBRARY
60 Winter St.
Keene, NH 03431
352-0157

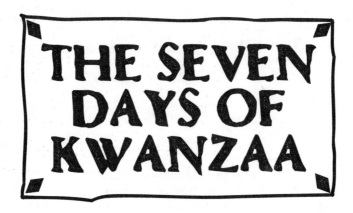

THE SEVEN DAYS OF KWANZAA

SCHOLASTIC INC.

New York Toronto London Auckland Sydney

To the Hawkins family, with love.

Cover art by Synthia St. James
Interior craft illustrations by Patricia B. A. Shea
Interiors designed by Jennifer Blanc/Neuwirth & Associates

ISBN 0-590-46360-8

12 11   8 9/9

Printed in the U.S.A.   40

First Scholastic printing, October 1994

CONTENTS

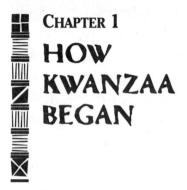

CHAPTER 1
HOW KWANZAA BEGAN

In August 1965, a riot erupted in Watts, a predominantly African-American community in Los Angeles, California. People in the community were angry about the crumbling houses, low-paying jobs, and racism they faced day after day. On August 11, the anger many African-Americans were feeling came to a boiling point.

A riot broke out when police officers arrested Marquette Frye, an African-American motorist. Some bystanders felt that Frye was treated too roughly by the police. During the long, hot August night that followed, police and passing cars were bombarded with bricks, bottles, and slabs of concrete.

The riot continued for the next four days.

Four thousand people were arrested, hundreds were injured, thirty-four were killed. Cars were overturned. Windows were broken. Many buildings in the community were looted and set on fire, and the smoke from the flames could be seen for miles around. Police sirens wailed morning and night. There was more than two hundred million dollars' worth of property damage and loss.

When the riot was finally over, many places in the community were nothing but smoke and ashes. Hundreds of people were left homeless. Broken glass littered the sidewalks. Several businesses closed and moved to other locations. Watts looked like a war had been fought there.

But in the aftermath of the riot, something began to change in Watts. African-Americans in Watts and across the city, joined together with a purpose, to rebuild Watts and make the community stronger and better.

Maulana Karenga was finishing his last year of graduate school during the Watts riot. He, too, wanted to help rebuild Watts and bring African-Americans together.

Karenga felt his people had lost touch

with their African heritage. After receiving his PhD, he began teaching African-American history at California State University, Long Beach. He also began studying ways that African-Americans could help themselves and each other. He wanted to unify his people and instill in them a sense of pride in their culture. Dr. Karenga felt that there should be a special time during the year set aside for this purpose. He began to research ancient African harvest ceremonies, and "first fruit" celebrations.

Dr. Karenga studied the culture of the Yourbas, the Ibos, the Ashantis, the Zulus, and other African tribes. Although each tribe celebrated the harvest festival a little differently, there were many things the festivals had in common.

The harvest festival was a way of rewarding all the tribe members for their teamwork during the year. Seeds could not be planted, fields could not be tended, and crops could not be gathered unless the entire tribe worked together as a group. Everyone in the tribe, from the smallest child to the oldest adult had a job to do. By working together, the entire tribe had food to eat throughout the year.

The harvest festival usually lasted several

days. The king or chief said a prayer for the health and wealth of each tribe member. He also gave honor to the tribe's ancestors. Sometimes, a special cup was filled and passed around the group in memory of those who had died long ago. After the ceremony was over, there was feasting, music, and dancing all night long. The African harvest festival was a time for tribe members to remember their ancestors, celebrate good fortune, and plan for the new year to come.

In 1966, Dr. Karenga created Kwanzaa, a cultural holiday based upon the ancient customs of Africa. He added an "a" to the Swahili word for first, kwanza, to create the name for the holiday.

Now, on December 26, the day after Christmas, and until the new year begins, Kwanzaa is celebrated by many African-Americans. Some African-Americans observe Christmas and Kwanzaa, others simply celebrate Kwanzaa.

Kwanzaa is not a religious holiday or one that honors a heroic person. It is not a holiday that is celebrated in Africa. Kwanzaa is an original African-American holiday. Kwanzaa is a time when African-Americans join together to honor the traditions of their ancestors. Planning for the year to come and working on ways to make themselves a better people and their community a better community are important parts of the holiday. Kwanzaa is a celebration of the past, the present, and the future.

Dr. Karenga also incorporated many African customs, traditions, symbols, and words from the Swahili language when he created Kwanzaa. Swahili is a nontribal African language that is spoken in East Africa and many other areas across the continent. Many Swahili words and phrases like *"Habari gani?"* (What's the news?) and *"Harambee!"* (Let's pull together!) are used as part of the Kwanzaa celebration. All of the words and symbols used during Kwanzaa are defined in the last chapter of this book.

Dr. Karenga also established a special set of goals called the *Nguzo Saba* to be memorized, discussed, and acted upon during the seven days of Kwanzaa, and throughout the year. The *Nguzo Saba* means "seven principles" in Swahili. These are the *Nguzo Saba* principles:

UMOJA (unity): To work together in peace with our family, our community, our nation, and our race.

KUJICHAGULIA (self-determination): To make up our minds to accomplish the goals we have set for ourselves.

UJIMA (collective work and responsibility): To team together to solve problems and to make our community a safe and productive place.

UJAMAA (cooperative economics): To build and maintain our own stores, shops, and other businesses and profit from them together.

NIA (purpose): To have a plan for the future and to be willing to help others to succeed as well.

KUUMBA (creativity): To always do as much as we can, in any way we can, in order to leave our community a better and more beautiful place.

IMANI (faith): To believe with all our heart in our people, our parents, our teachers, our leaders, and the righteousness and victory of our struggle.

Dr. Karenga hoped that the things that were studied and practiced during Kwanzaa would guide African-Americans all year long. There is a proverb that is often quoted during the Kwanzaa celebration: "I am because we are, because we are, I am."

The principles, symbols, and ceremonies that are a part of Kwanzaa celebrate the beauty of working together as one for the good of the community. *Harambee!*

CHAPTER 2:
CELEBRATING KWANZAA

Kwanzaa is a festive occasion, a special time spent with family and with friends. It is a time of great rejoicing, but also a time to quietly think about our lives and the future. One of the things to remember about Kwanzaa is that it should be celebrated in a way that its principles will be most meaningful not only during the holiday, but in the years to come.

There is a traditional way of celebrating Kwanzaa. A few basic items are needed to begin. The black, red, and green *bendera ya taifa* flag and a poster of the *Nguzo Saba*, the seven principles, are displayed. A table is set with a straw mat called a *mkeka*. The *mkeka* is a symbol of past traditions, and African-

American history. There is an African proverb that says, "No matter how high a house is built, it must stand on something." All the items used during the Kwanzaa celebration are placed on the *mkeka*.

Next, one black, three red, and three green candles called the *mishumaa saba* are placed in a candle holder called a *kinara*. Each candle stands for one of the seven principles of Kwanzaa. The black candle represents *umoja* (unity) and is placed in the center of the *kinara*. The black candle is lit during the first day of the celebration. The other candles are lit from left to right on the following days. The three red candles represent *nia*, (purpose), *kuumba* (creativity), and *imani* (faith). They are placed to the left of the black candle. The three green candles represent *kujichagulia* (self-determination), *ujima* (collective work and responsibility), and *ujamaa* (cooperative economics). They are placed to the right of the black candle.

A bowl of fruit and vegetables called *mazao,* and two or more ears of corn called *mihindi,* are placed on the *mkeka.* The fruit and vegetables represent the harvest, which is the reward for working together throughout

principle of the day is discussed. Everyone has a chance to explain what the *Nguzo Saba* principle means to them. After the discussion, everyone shouts, *"Harambee!"*

Harambee is shouted once on the first day of Kwanzaa. The number of times it is shouted increases until *harambee* is said seven times on the seventh day of the celebration, January 1.

Many African-Americans wear African-style clothing during the Kwanzaa celebration. Women often wear a beautiful, loose-fitting gown called a *buba,* or a robe with a scarf at the waist called a *busuti.* Some women cover their hair with a head wrap called a *gele.* A shirt called a *dashiki* can be worn by men or women. Women often wear a *lapa,* which is a cleverly wrapped length of cloth, as a skirt. A *kanza,* which is a long robe, is worn by many men.

Some adults do not eat anything from sunrise until sunset during Kwanzaa as a way of purifying their minds and bodies. That evening, a wonderful meal is prepared and enjoyed by all, and afterward the candle-lighting ceremony begins. In some cities, a celebration is held at a different location for each day of Kwanzaa. Some families join in the community-wide gathering after celebrating their candle-lighting ceremony at home.

On the sixth day of Kwanzaa, December 31, the *karamu* is held. The *karamu* feast is a gathering of family and friends.

The place where the *karamu* feast is held is decorated in a beautiful black, red, and green color scheme. A *kinara* and *mkeka* are placed in the room and are used as part of the ceremony during the feast. The meal is often served African-style with pillows or cushions arranged around low tables, or a traditional seating arrangement may be used. *Zawadi* gifts are exchanged.

In keeping with the spirit of Kwanzaa, creativity is shown by giving *zawadi* (handmade) gifts. Gifts which are purchased are designed to improve the mind and heart of the person who receives them. The most commonly purchased gifts are books written about Africa and African-American culture or history. The gifts are opened on the first day of the new year.

The feast begins with a speech called the *kukaribisha,* which is usually given by one of the older people. Special guests are recognized at this time.

Sometimes, guests are given a chance to express what a principle of the *Nguzo Saba* means to them. One by one, the guests light a candle and speak about the principle the candle represents. This is called the *kukumbuka*.

After the candle-lighting ceremony, there is a time for stories, songs, dances, skits, and other performances. They occur throughout the *karamu* program.

Next, the *kuchunguza tena na kutoa ahadi tena* begins. This is the time for the guests to recommit themselves to the principles learned during Kwanzaa. Sometimes a guest speaker gives a speech. Then the *kushangilia* (rejoicing) begins. Group songs are one way of rejoicing during the Kwanzaa feast.

After the rejoicing, the *tamshi la tambiko* (libation statement) is recited.

This is a modern libation statement:

For the Motherland cradle of civilization.
For the ancestors and their indomitable spirit.
For the elders from whom we can learn much.
For our youth who represent the promise for tomorrow.
For our people the original people.
For our struggle and in remembrance of those

18

who have struggled on our behalf.
For umoja the principle of unity,
which should guide us in all that we do.
For the creator who provides all things great and small.

After the libation statement, the *kikombe cha umoja* (unity cup) is filled with water. Water is used because it is the essence of life. The water pitcher is held up in the direction of the four winds: north, south, east, and west. Then the cup is filled and passed around to each person. Everyone makes a sipping gesture in honor of the ancestors. Sometimes, a small amount of water is poured directly onto the floor in remembrance of those who are dead.

When the cup has been passed to everyone and is placed back on the table, the *kutoa majina* (calling out of the names of family ancestors and African-American heroes) begins, as a way of remembering them. When the last name has been called, the *ngoma* (drums) begin. A drummer plays African-style rhythms or a recording of African drum songs is played. This is a signal for the start of the *karamu* feast.

At some Kwanzaa celebrations, everyone

brings a dish for the feast. Sharing food is symbolic of the way our African ancestors shared their harvest. When the feast is held in someone's home, the host may prefer to prepare all the food.

After the feast, the singing, dancing, and stories continue, sometimes all night.

When the *karamu* celebration ends, the *tamshi la tutaonana* (farewell statement) is made. This is part of a farewell statement composed by Dr. Karenga:

> "Strive for discipline, dedication and achievement in all you do. Dare struggle and sacrifice and gain the strength that comes from this. Build where you are and dare leave a legacy that will last as long as the sun shines and the water flows...May the year's end meet us laughing and stronger."

At the end of the farewell statement, everyone shouts *Harambee!* seven times and the feast is over.

The seventh and last day of Kwanzaa is *imani.* It is the first day of the new year. *Zawadi* gifts which have been received can now be opened. Then, the rest of the day is spent in reflection and recommitment to the *Nguzo Saba.*

Imani is also a time for planning ways to make the new year ahead better than the old. The new year is the time to put into action the principles that were learned during Kwanzaa, and to continue the struggle to rescue and reconstruct the community. Let's all pull together! *Harambee! Harambee! Harambee!*

Chapter 4:

PREPARING A KWANZAA KARAMU FEAST

Family and friends join together on the evening of the sixth day of Kwanzaa to create a meal in a joyous celebration of the holiday. The feast is also a reminder of the way our African ancestors gathered together to share the fruits of their harvest.

These unknown ancestors were taken as slaves, along with millions of others primarily from the coasts of West, East, and South Africa. They were sold into slavery in the Caribbean, South America, and North America.

The captives introduced the African way of cooking into the menus of every country where they were enslaved. African slaves introduced four main foods into the American diet—okra, which they called *gombo*; sesame seeds which they called *benne* and the oil it produces; cowpeas or black-eyed peas; and peanuts, which they called ground nuts or goobers. Most of the African names for these foods are still used today. The seedlings for these foods were often transported from Africa by slave ships. Some of the herbs and spices that are now commonly used in American cooking can be traced back to Africa.

The *karamu* feast is celebrated in the spirit of our ancestors, with joy, lots of good food, music, and unity. *Harambee! Harambee! Harambee! Harambee!*

Rules to Remember

The recipes that are included in this chapter are fun and easy to prepare. There are a few simple rules to remember before you begin to cook. Always work with an adult.

1. If you are not sure about the measurements required in a recipe, or if you do not understand the directions, ask an adult to help you.

2. Always check to make sure you have all the ingredients listed in the recipe before you begin.

3. Set out all the ingredients and utensils you need.

4. Wash your hands before handling any food.

5. Wash all fruits and vegetables you use. Chop, shred, or grate recipe ingredients first.

6. Remember, if you are using sharp utensils, to be careful not to cut yourself, or ask an adult to cut the items for you. Always cut in the direction away from your fingers and hands. Use a clean cutting board.

7. If you are removing hot dishes from the stovetop or oven, use oven mitts to protect your hands or ask an adult to remove the dish for you.

8. Turn pot handles toward the back of the stove to prevent accidents.

9. Be careful that oven mitts, dish towels, aprons, clothing, hair, ribbons, or other items on your body are not near an open flame.

10. Ask for adult permission and assistance when using any kitchen appliance, such as microwaves, blenders, ovens, mixers, can openers, etc.

MENU FOR A KWANZAA KARAMU FEAST

North African Orange Salad
Ashanti Peanut Soup
Gambian Fish Caldou
Okra with Corn
Ugandan Spinach and Sesame Seeds
Black-eyed Peas and Rice (Hoppin' John)
Baked Sweet Potatoes with Spiced Butter
Liberian Rice Bread
Caribbean Fruit Punch
Senegalese Cookies

❖ NORTH AFRICAN ❖ ORANGE SALAD

UTENSILS: Knife, cutting board, measuring spoons, salad fork and spoon, or two forks, small mixing bowl, salad bowl

- 2 large oranges, peeled and sliced thin
- 2 cups lettuce, shredded
- 1 large onion, peeled and sliced thin
- 8 Greek olives, pitted and sliced
- 2 tablespoons olive oil
- 2 tablespoons lemon juice
- 1/8 teaspoon salt
- 1/8 teaspoon pepper

Using a salad fork and spoon, or two dinner forks, mix the lettuce, onions, and olives together in a salad bowl. Arrange orange slices on top. Mix oil, lemon juice, salt, and pepper together in a small bowl to make a salad dressing. Pour dressing over salad. Refrigerate. Serves 4.

❖ ASHANTI PEANUT SOUP ❖

Peanuts are called groundnuts in Africa. African captives introduced the peanut to American cooking. African-American scientist Dr. George Washington Carver experimented with the peanut to see if it could be grown as an alternative to cotton in the South. His research developed more than three hundred different products that could be made from peanuts! Dr. Carver used peanuts in everything from paint to peanut butter. Once, Dr. Carver invited several prominent people to dinner. After eating the delicious meal, his guests were amazed to learn that everything from the "meat" to the dessert was made from peanuts!

This recipe is a popular one in West Africa.

UTENSILS: Measuring cup and spoons, grater, knife, cutting board, small mixing bowl, heavy saucepan, long-handled mixing spoon, oven mitts, blender

2   teaspoons flour
3   cups milk
3   cups chicken broth (canned broth is fine)
2   cups crunchy peanut butter
2   tablespoons grated onion
1/4   cup chopped parsley
1/2   teaspoon salt
1/2   teaspoon pepper

Mix the flour and milk together in a bowl. Stir until the mixture is smooth. Pour the mixture into a heavy saucepan. Add the chicken broth, peanut butter, onion, parsley, salt, and pepper. Stir all the ingredients together. Turn the heat up to bring the soup to a boil. As soon as the soup begins to boil, turn the heat down to low. Let the soup simmer for fifteen minutes over low heat. Stir often.

When the soup has finished cooking, cover your hands with oven mitts and carefully pour the soup into a blender. Blend for three minutes. Pour the soup into individual bowls. Serve the soup while it is hot. Serves 6.

❖ GAMBIAN FISH CALDOU ❖

UTENSILS: measuring cup and spoons, grater, knife, heavy skillet with a lid, spatula, platter, spoon

- 6 one-inch-thick fillets of mild, white-fleshed fish (such as bass, catfish, cod, orange roughy, salmon, tuna, sole, trout, or flounder)
- 1/2 cup water
- 1/8 teaspoon red pepper
- 1 large onion, grated
- 1 bay leaf
- 1 teaspoon salt

Gently rinse fish fillets under cold running water. Place the fish in a heavy skillet. Add the water, red pepper, grated onion, bay leaf, and salt. Turn the heat up. When the water starts to boil, turn the heat down to low. Cover the pan with the lid. Cook fish for eight minutes. Fish is done when it is flaky but not mushy. The bay leaf is only used for seasoning and may be thrown away after the fish is done.

Carefully remove fish from pan with a large spatula and place the fish onto a platter. Slowly spoon the liquid remaining in the pan over the fish. Serve the fish while it is hot. Serves 4–6.

❖ BLACK-EYED PEAS ❖ AND RICE (HOPPIN' JOHN)

Black-eyed peas were called cowpeas in Africa. The peas were transported from Africa to the West Indies and then into the Carolinas before the early 1700s. Black-eyed peas are said to bring good luck in the New Year. Hoppin' John is an African dish that has been adapted for American tastes. It is commonly served on New Year's Day.

UTENSILS: measuring cup and spoons, knife, 5-quart saucepan with a lid, spoon, oven mitt

    1   (10-ounce) package frozen black-eyed peas
    4   cups plus 1/2 cup of water
  1/4   teaspoon salt
    2   cups white rice
    1   small onion, diced
    4   tablespoons margarine or butter

Pour 1/2 cup water into a 5-quart saucepan. Place frozen black-eyed peas and salt in water. Turn heat to high. Cover the pot and bring it to a boil.

32

Cover your hand with an oven mitt and carefully remove the cover from the pot so that the steam does not burn you. Pour in the remaining 4 cups of water, the rice, onion, and margarine or butter. Stir. Cover the pot and return water to a boil.

Turn the heat to low. Cook the black-eyed peas and rice for twenty minutes. Do not remove cover.

After twenty minutes, remove cover and stir the peas and rice with a fork. If the peas and rice are not tender, and all the water is not absorbed, cover and continue to cover for another five minutes. Serve black-eyed peas and rice with Gambian Fish Caldou (see page 29.) Serves 6.

❖ LIBERIAN RICE BREAD ❖

Liberia was originally settled by newly freed slaves in the 1800s. The name Liberia comes from the Latin word *liber*, which means free. This is a popular recipe in that country.

UTENSILS: measuring cup and spoons, mixer, large mixing bowl, wooden mixing spoon or plastic spatula, 8 x 12-inch rectangular or 9-inch round cake pan, oven mitts

- 2 cups cream of rice cereal
- 4 tablespoons sugar
- 1 teaspoon baking soda
- 1 teaspoon salt
- 1/2 teaspoon nutmeg
- 3 cups mashed bananas
- 1 cup water
- 1/2 cup vegetable oil

Preheat oven to 400° F. In a large mixing bowl, mix together by hand or with a mixer, the cream of rice cereal, sugar, baking soda, salt, and nutmeg until well blended. Add the bananas, water, and vegetable oil. Stir until mixture is smooth, about three minutes.

Spoon batter into 8 x 12-inch rectangular or 9-inch round cake pan. Bake for thirty minutes or until lightly browned. Cover your hands with oven mitts. Remove bread from oven and serve hot with butter or margarine.

❖ CARIBBEAN ❖ FRUIT PUNCH

UTENSILS: measuring cup, long-handled spoon, large pitcher or punch bowl

    2 1/2 cups lemonade
    1 cup orange juice
    1 cup pineapple juice
    1 cup papaya juice
    1 cup guava juice

Mix all the juices together in a large pitcher or punch bowl. Serve punch over ice.

showing *kuumba* (creativity) and is in the
true spirit of Kwanzaa. *Harambee! Harambee!
Harambee! Harambee!   Harambee!*

A MKEKA MAT

A *mkeka* is a woven
mat. In Africa, it is made
out of straw. During
Kwanzaa, the *mkeka* is a
symbol of the foundation
that African-American
traditions are built upon.
You can make a *mkeka*
out of newspaper.

THINGS YOU WILL NEED

10–12 sheets of
newspaper
stapler
acrylic or poster paint
paintbrush
glue
water

MAKING A *MKEKA* MAT

1. Take a single sheet of newspaper and, starting at the
shorter end, fold the
newspaper over two
inches. Smooth the
paper flat and continue
folding it over two inches at
a time until it reaches the
middle of the page.

8. Now that you have finished making your mat, you are ready to paint it. You can use either acrylic or poster paint. You might want to paint your *mkeka* red, black, and green, which are the colors of Kwanzaa. After the paint has dried, you can preserve your *mkeka* by mixing 1/2 cup of glue with 1/2 cup of water. Paint the mixture on both sides of the mat and let it dry.

WEAVING CLOTH TO MAKE A BELT

The people of Ghana, West Africa, are famous for their woven cloth. The woven patterns of the cloth vary from tribe to tribe. *Kente*, which is made of silken threads in a rainbow of colors, is one type of cloth that is woven in Ghana.

In Ghana, men usually use small, portable looms that they can carry from village to village. They trade the 4- to 6-inch strips of cloth for food and other supplies. Larger pieces of woven cloth are usually crafted by women. They use heavy looms capable of turning out squares of woven fabric about 16 x 20 inches wide. After the cloth has been woven, the strips are sewn together to make clothing, carpets, or blankets.

You can make a simple loom to weave a strip of cloth that can be worn as a belt.

1. Cut four pieces of yarn, each 80 inches long.

2. Then cut 1/2 inch off the

THINGS YOU WILL NEED

4 plastic straws
1 skein 4-ply
worsted yarn
scissors

AFRICAN TOE PUPPETS

African toe puppets became popular in Mozambique and the Ivory Coast in the 1940s and 1950s. The puppets were made from pieces of bamboo with tufts of lion fur for hair. Vegetable twine was used to attach the puppets to the puppeteer's toes. Using the big toes to move the puppets left the puppeteer's hands free to move while he sang, played an instrument, or

THINGS YOU WILL NEED
Cardboard tubes (toilet paper tubes are fine or you may cut a paper towel tube in half) fake fur or yarn glue cardboard brads or pipe cleaners two 12-inch pieces of string, plus four 4-inch pieces empty thread spools, buttons or beads

told a story. The taller puppet represented the male and the shorter one, the female. You can make up your own stories and songs to tell or sing while your toe puppets dance.

1. Draw a face on the cardboard tube.

2. Glue a tuft of the fake fur or yarn on one end of the tube to represent hair.

49

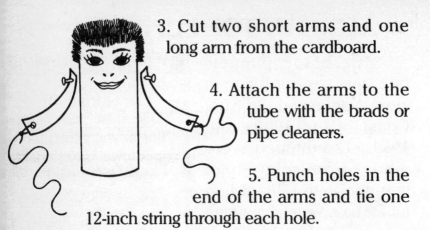

3. Cut two short arms and one long arm from the cardboard.

4. Attach the arms to the tube with the brads or pipe cleaners.

5. Punch holes in the end of the arms and tie one 12-inch string through each hole.

6. String an empty thread spool, beads, or buttons on the 4-inch strings. Tie a knot on the ends.

7. Punch holes on the bottom end of the tubes. Thread string through holes to attach the spool, button, or bead "legs."

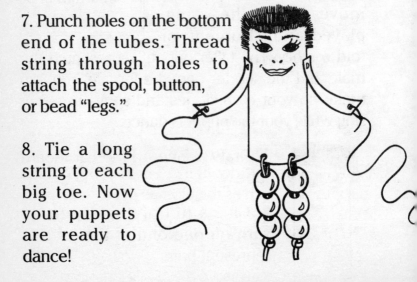

8. Tie a long string to each big toe. Now your puppets are ready to dance!

MAKING A
TIE-DYED GELE

A *gele* is a two-yard length of cloth about 10 to 15 inches wide. Many African women wear a *gele*. Tie-dying fabric is an ancient craft using knots, strings, pleats, and other creases in the cloth to produce a design when the fabric is dyed. A tie-dyed *gele* makes a beautiful zawadi gift. Tie-dying is simple but very messy. Ask an adult to help you with the dying process.

THINGS YOU WILL NEED
2 yards of cotton fabric, 10 to 15 inches wide
cord
masking tape
rubber bands
fabric dye

1. Accordion pleat the cloth in 2–to 4–inch folds at regular intervals lengthwise.

2. Wrap the cord, masking tape, or rubber bands around the pleated fabric tightly, in intervals down the length of the fabric, to make a pattern as the cloth is dyed.

51

3. Carefully follow the instructions on the package of fabric dye.

4. When your fabric has been dyed and is dry, remove the cord, masking tape, or rubber bands. Now your *gele* is ready to wear!

How to Wrap a *Gele*

1. Stand in front of a mirror. Hold the *gele* so that the back of your head is in the center of the fabric. Hold the ends of the fabric in each hand. The two sides should be even when you bring the fabric up to the top of your head.

2. Holding the ends of the fabric, bring the two sides forward and overlap them in the front. Wrap the loose ends around to the back of your head.

3. Tie the fabric in a comfortable knot near the base of the back of your head.

4. Bring the loose ends back to the front of your head and cross them.

5. Pleat the fabric and tuck the ends into the folds in the front or sides of your *gele.* Or you

may tuck the end of one side into the top of the *gele*, and drape the other side loosely behind your ear.

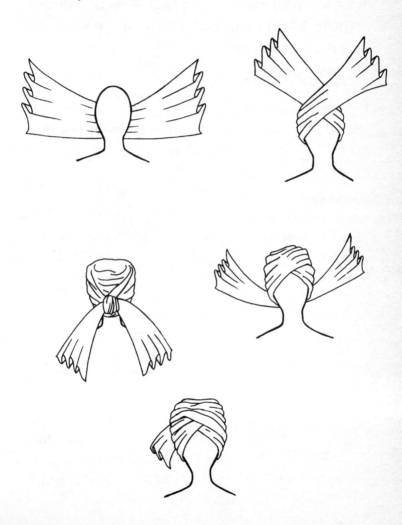

ZAWADI JEWELRY

African craftspeople have been making jewelry for hundreds of years. This is a simple way to make a necklace or bracelet to be given as a *zawadi* gift.

THINGS YOU WILL NEED

2 boxes of large
ziti noodles
tempera paints (red,
black, green, and other
colors)
paintbrushes
glitter, beads, or buttons
tennis shoelaces (different
lengths)
wax paper

1. Paint the noodles with the tempera paint.

2. Sprinkle the wet noodles with glitter, if desired.

3. Lay the wet noodles on sheets of wax paper to dry, about one hour.

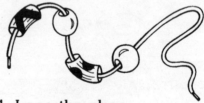

4. Lace the shoe-laces through the noodles, beads, and buttons in an attractive design. Use short laces for bracelets and long ones for necklaces. Now your *zawadi* jewelry is ready to give as a gift.

MAKING AN OWARE GAME

Oware is a popular game in many regions of Africa. It is called Mankala in parts of East Africa; Ayo, Wari, or Oware in the west, and Ohoro in the southern part of Africa. All of these names mean "transferring." Oware is played by moving or transferring nuts, stones, or beans, which are called hasa, from one cup to another until there are no more left to move. The winner is the one who has the most playing pieces at the end of the game.

In some tribes, only kings are allowed to play Oware. Everyone else watches. Many Oware boards are beautifully carved and decorated. In some parts of Africa, twelve holes are scooped out of the sand, and the game is played with stones.

Oware is usually played in the afternoon when it is too hot to work. You can make your own Oware game using things you have around the house.

THINGS YOU WILL NEED

2 egg cartons
markers, crayons, paint, and white paper
tape
48 dried beans, marbles, buttons, stones, or pebbles

---

1. Cut off two of the cups on one of the egg cartons and throw the rest of the carton away.

2. Attach one cup to each end of the remaining egg carton with the tape. These cups remain empty until you start to play. The end cups are used to hold the winning game pieces.

3. Decorate the paper with African drawings and symbols. Tape the paper to the top of the egg carton.

4. Place four playing pieces in each of the twelve cups of the egg carton. Now you are ready to play Oware!

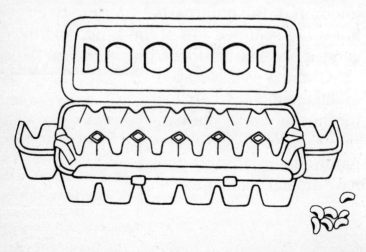

OWARE GAME RULES

Place the Oware game so that each player has six cups in front of her. The first player picks up four beans from any of the cups on her left. She drops one bean in each cup, going counterclockwise, in a circle to her left, until all the beans in her hand are gone. The second player does the same thing. If a player drops her last bean in a cup with at least two or more beans in it, she wins all the beans in that cup. She puts her winnings in her cup at the end of the board.

The game continues until there are no more beans left in any of the twelve cups. Each player counts the beans in their end cups. The one with the most beans wins.

Chapter 6:
SEVEN CELEBRATION STORIES

The seven biographies contained in this chapter are about famous African-American men or women. Like an African *griot* or storyteller, each person relates the story of their life in their own words. Each biography represents a principle from the *Nguzo Saba*: *umoja* (unity), *kujichagulia* (self-determination), *ujima* (collective work and responsibility), *ujamaa* (cooperative economics), *nia* (purpose), *kuumba* (creativity), and *imani* (faith). Reading these stories during the Kwanzaa holiday helps to illustrate the meaning of the *Nguzo Saba* principle for that day. *Harambee! Harambee! Harambee! Harambee! Harambee! Harambee!*

Umoja (unity): To work together peacefully with our family, our community, our nation, and our race.

SHEYANN WEB'S STORY
Walk Together Children

In 1965, Sheyann Webb was an eight-year-old elementary school student in Selma, Alabama. One day, on her way to school, Sheyann had a chance to meet Dr. Martin Luther King, Jr., a leader of the movement for

African-American civil rights. Dr. King was in Selma to unite the African-American community to fight against racism. For the first time, Sheyann saw African-Americans from all walks of life working together for a cause— equal rights. Sheyann joined the protest movement. She became a song leader during the rallies Dr. King held to organize African-Americans to register to vote. King believed that once African-Americans could vote, they could change the laws in the South that discriminated against them.

Of the 15,000 African-Americans who lived in Selma, only 355 were registered to vote. Sometimes blacks would have to stand in line all day, waiting for the voter registration office to open. Then, after hours of waiting, the registrar would say that the office would not be open that day. On other days, only one or two of the hundreds of African-Americans who were standing in line would be allowed to register. Then the office would close until the next morning.

During this time, thirty-eight hundred protesters had been arrested, and only fifty African-Americans had been allowed to sign up to vote. Protest marches were organized to bring attention to Selma's discrimination against blacks. During one march, twenty-five-year-old Jimmy Lee Jackson was shot and killed. Jackson was trying to protect his mother who was being beaten by a state trooper.

King met with President Lyndon Baines Johnson on March 5, 1965. He complained to the president about the harsh treatment of African-Americans in the South, and asked the president to pass the Voting Rights Act. This act would add support to the Civil Rights Acts that had been passed previously.

After meeting with the president, King began organizing a protest march in memory of Jimmy Lee Jackson. The march was to start in Selma, Alabama, and end at the state capital, in Montgomery, Alabama, about fifty miles away.

Alabama's governor, George Wallace, forbade the march and ordered state troopers to stop the protesters. King was unable to lead the march, so Hosea Williams and John Lewis, two civil rights workers, took charge in his absence. Protesters of all ages were a part of the march, including Sheyann Webb.

March 7, 1965, the date of the first Selma to Montgomery march, has gone down in history as Bloody Sunday. Alabama state troopers blocked the marchers path and gave them three minutes to turn around. Some of the protesters knelt to pray. Then, after about sixty seconds, state troopers, mounted on horses and wearing gas masks, charged into the marchers. Tear gas filled the air and the horses trampled over the defenseless marchers. This is Sheyann Webb's story:

All I knew is I heard all this screaming and the people were turning and I saw this first part of the line running and stumbling back toward us. At that point, I was just off the bridge and on the side of the highway. And they came running and some of them were crying out. There were people everywhere, jamming against me, pushing against me. Then, all of a sudden, it stopped and everyone got down on their knees, and I did, too, and somebody was saying for us to pray. But there was so much excitement it never got started, because everybody was talking and they were scared and we didn't know what was happening or was going to happen. It seemed like just a few seconds went by and I heard a shout. "Gas! Gas!" And everybody started screaming again. And I looked and I saw the troopers charging us again and some of them were swinging their arms and throwing canisters of tear gas. And beyond them I saw the horsemen starting their charge toward us. I was terrified. What happened then is something I'll never forget as long as I live. Never. In fact, I still dream about it sometimes.

I saw those horsemen coming toward me and they had those awful masks on; they rode right through the cloud of tear gas. People were running and falling and ducking, and you could hear the horses' hooves on the pavement and you'd hear the whips swishing and you'd hear them striking the people. Women as well as men were getting hit. I never got hit, but one of the horses went right by me and I heard the swish sound as the whip went over my head and cracked some man across the back. It seem to take forever to get across the bridge.

The troopers chased the protesters back to Brown's Chapel, the starting place of the march. Some of the troopers rode their horses through the church. Fifty people were treated for cuts, bruises, and other injuries. Seventy more were taken to the hospital.

Later that evening, the protesters sat in shocked silence at the chapel. The state troopers still remained outside the building.

It was like we were at our own funeral. But then later in the night, maybe nine-thirty or ten, I don't know for sure, all of a sudden somebody there started humming. I think they were moaning and it just went into the humming of a freedom song. It was real low, but some of us children began humming along, slow and soft. At first I didn't even know what it was, what song, I mean. It was like a funeral sound, a dirge. Then I recognized it—"Ain't Gonna Let Nobody Turn Me 'Round." I'd never heard it or hummed it that way before. But it just started to catch on, and the people began to pick it up. It started to swell, the humming. Then we began singing the words. We sang, "Ain't gonna let George Wallace turn me 'round." And, "Ain't gonna let Jim Clark [County Sheriff] turn me 'round." "Ain't gonna let no state trooper turn me 'round. Ain't gonna let no horses…ain't gonna let no tear gas—ain't gonna let nobody turn me 'round. Nobody!"

…We was singing and telling the world that we hadn't been whipped, that we had won. Just all of a sudden something happened that night and we knew in that church that—Lord Almighty—we had really won after all. We had won!

The suffering and death that happened in Selma moved the nation to protest the mistreatment of African-Americans in the South. On August 6, 1965, President Johnson signed the Voting Rights Act. The protesters had won!

Kujichagulia (self-determination): To make up our mind to accomplish the goals we have set for ourselves.

WILMA RUDOLPH'S STORY
Running to Find Myself

Wilma Rudolph was born in Clarksville, Tennessee, in 1940. She was a sickly child. The doctors told her parents that she would never walk. Wilma not only learned to walk, she ran her way into the history books. She became one of the fastest women in the world during her track career.

Wilma faced many obstacles in her life, sickness, poverty, and the birth of her first child at eighteen. After her daughter was born, many felt that her track career was over. Wilma was determined to come back, and she did. Faster than ever. This is her story.

...I was six years old before I realized that there was something wrong with me. I was six and I still wasn't going to school. Now, you're six, and you're supposed to be in school like the other kids. But I did have this crooked left leg, and my left foot was turned inward. It didn't hurt me physically, and the only times anybody noticed it was when I was out playing with the other kids, and some of them would start teasing me and calling me "cripple."

My mother had mentioned a couple of times that I had been born with polio, but I didn't know what polio was, and besides, all I had was this crooked leg.

I was a premature baby, which meant I was born before my time. I was the most sickly kid in all of Clarksville [Tennessee]. I had double pneumonia twice. I had scarlet fever. I had whooping cough. I had a tonsillectomy. I had an appendectomy. In between, it seemed I always had a cold or a running nose or the sniffles. It was like I spent the first decade of my life being sick.

The brace went on my right leg when I was five, and I lived with that thing for the next half-dozen years. It was a steel brace, and it hooked onto my leg just above the knee and went all the way down my leg and connected to my shoe. The brace was supposed to keep the leg straight all the time and prevent me from walking on the leg sideways. I used to put it on as soon as I got up in the morning and I wasn't allowed to take it off until I went to bed that night...It weighed a couple of pounds and it looked so terrible; it always reminded me that something was wrong with me. Psychologically, wearing that brace was devastating.

I was nine-and-a-half years old when I took off the brace and went out in public without it. I'll never forget it. I went to church, and walked in without the brace, and I knew right off that people were looking at me, saying to themselves, "Hey, there's Wilma, and she doesn't have the brace on her leg anymore." ...I just smiled and beamed, and didn't say much. But looking back on it, I'd say it was one of the most important moments of my life. From that day on, people were going to start separating me from that brace, start thinking about me differently, start saying that Wilma is a healthy kid, just like all the rest of them.

After the scarlet fever and the whooping cough, I remember I started to get mad about it all. I got angry. I went through the stage of asking myself, "Wilma, what is this existence all about? Is it about being sick all the time? It can't be." So I started getting angry about things, fighting back in a new way, with a vengeance. I think I started acquiring a competitive spirit right then and there, a spirit that would make me successful in sports later on. I was mad, and I was going to beat these illnesses no matter what. No more taking what comes, no more drifting off, no more wondering. Enough was enough.

Wilma grew up to become a healthy teenager with a passionate love for sports. She was an all-state high school basketball champion at fifteen, scoring 803 points in twenty-five games. In 1960, she qualified for the summer Olympics in Rome, Italy. Wilma ran the 100-meter dash, the 200-meter dash, and the 440-meter relay.

On Friday, the 440 relay was scheduled. That was my chance to become the first American woman ever to win three Olympic gold medals. I wasn't about to blow it. The team was: Martha Hudson, running the first leg; Barbara Jones, running the second; Lucinda Williams, running the third; and me, running anchor. The teams everybody was talking about were Russia, West Germany, and Britain. Well, we wiped them all out, and we set a world's record!

When I broke the tape; I had my three gold medals, and the feeling of accomplishment welled up inside me. The first American woman to win three Olympic gold medals! I knew that was something nobody could ever take away from me, ever.

Ujima (collective work and responsibility):
To team together to solve problems and to make our
community a safe and productive place.

IDA B. WELLS-BARNETT'S STORY
Tell My People to Go West

Ida B. Wells-Barnett was six months old when slavery ended in 1863. She spent her life working on ways to make the African-American community a stronger one. Ida began her working career at the age of sixteen as a teacher in Holly Springs, Mississippi. She also worked part-time as a reporter for the Negro Press Association. Ida wrote truthfully and forcefully about issues that affected the African-American community. One of Ida's articles was about the poor school buildings, books, and equipment that African-American children were given. After reading the article, the school board fired her. Ida continued writing and went on to become a full-time newspaper editor and owner of the Memphis, Tennessee, *Free Speech and Headlight*. Her policy was to always tell the truth, no matter what.

In 1892, something happened that would change Ida's life forever. Thomas Moss, Calvin McDowell, and Henry Stewart were threatened by a white mob because their store, People's Grocery, was far more success-ful than a white-owned store in the same neighborhood. After hearing about the threats, members of the African-American community armed themselves. They stood guard at the People's Grocery to protect their neighbor's property. When three white men broke into the rear of the store, they were fired on and wounded. Moss, McDowell, and Stewart were arrested and jailed, along with hundreds of other African-American male "suspects."

One morning, a mob took Moss, McDowell, and Stewart from their cells and hung them. Before he died, Moss was asked if there was anything he wanted to say. "Tell my people to go west," Moss said. "There is no justice for them here."

Wells was out of town when the murders occurred. When she returned, she wrote an article for her newspaper that would change her life. This is that story.

The city of Memphis has demonstrated that neither character nor standing avails the Negro if he dares to protect himself against the white man or becomes his rival. There is nothing we can do about the lynchings now, as we are outnumbered and without arms. The white mob could help itself to ammunition without pay, but the order was rigidly enforced against the selling of guns to Negroes. There is therefore only one thing left that we can do; save our money and leave a town that will neither protect our lives and property, nor give us a fair trial in the courts, but takes us out and murders us in cold blood when accused by white persons.

The advice contained in the *Free Speech*, coupled with the last words of Thomas Moss, was taken up and re-echoed among our people throughout Memphis. Hundreds disposed of their property and left. Reverend R. N. Countee and Reverend W. A. Brinkley, both leading pastors, took their whole congregations with them as they, too, went west. Memphis had never seen such an upheaval among colored people.

Every time word came of people leaving Memphis, we who were left behind rejoiced. Oklahoma was about to be opened up and scores sold or gave away property, shook Memphis dust off their feet, and went out west as Tom Moss had said for us to do.

Ida was visiting New York when a mob wrecked her newspaper office and chased her business partner, J. L. Fleming, out of town. A note that was left behind stated, "Anyone trying to publish the paper again would be punished with death." Ida's friends begged her to stay in New York where she would be safe.

Although I had been warned repeatedly by my own people that something would happen if I did not cease harping on the lynchings of three months before, I had expected that happening to come when I was at home. My friends declared that the trains and my home were being watched by white men who promised to kill me on sight. They also told me that colored men were organized to protect me if I should return. They said it would mean more bloodshed, more widows and orphans if I came back, and now that I was out of it all, to stay away where I would be safe from harm.

Because I saw the chance to be of more service to the cause by staying in New York than by returning to Memphis, I accepted their advice, took a position on the *New York Age*, and continued my fight against lynching and lynchers. They had destroyed my paper, in which every dollar I had in the world was invested. They had made me an exile and threatened my life for hinting at the truth. I felt that I owed it to myself and my race to tell the whole truth.

Ida devoted the rest of her life to investigating and speaking out against lynchings. In 1895, she published *The Red Record*, a book which gave names, dates, and information about the murders of African-Americans. Ida spoke out against the murders around the world, and was one of the founding members of the National Association for the Advancement of Colored People. Ida also formed the first African-American women's clubs. These clubs, which were named in her honor, worked for women's rights and to better the conditions of African-American families around the Untied States. Ida continued to work on behalf of the African-American community until the day she died on March 25, 1931 at the age of sixty-nine.

Ujamaa (cooperative economics): To build and maintain our own stores, shops, and other businesses and profit from them together.

BENJAMIN "PAP" SINGLETON'S STORY
A Place of Our Own

Benjamin "Pap" Singleton was born into slavery in 1809 in Nashville, Tennessee. Singleton ran away constantly and was sold many times. He finally escaped to Canada and later made a home for himself in Detroit, Michigan. Singleton ran a boardinghouse and often hid fugitive slaves. When the Civil War brought an end to slavery, Singleton returned to Tennessee.

Life after slavery was still hard for many blacks in the South. Most worked under conditions only a little better than slavery. Along with the hard life the newly freed African-Americans led, crops were bad, many were homeless, there had been a yellow fever epidemic, and black women had been cruelly abused.

Singleton felt his "God-given mission" was to guarantee that all African-Americans had a safe home and decent way to make a living. Singleton wanted his people to own their own homes, lands, and businesses. He began urging them to buy farmland in Tennessee. The white landowners in Tennessee either refused to sell their land or set the prices too high.

In the early 1870s, Singleton, along with Columbus Johnson and A. D. DeFrantz, began searching for land in Kansas. Several African-American families from Tennessee had moved there in the late 1860s. Singleton thought

Kansas might be a good place for an African-American settlement. He visited Kansas in 1873 and found there were many jobs available and a large amount of unsettled land. Singleton returned to Kansas later that year, along with three hundred other African-Americans. They founded Singleton's Colony and Nicodemus Colony, and many settled in Cherokee and Dunlap counties, as well as Topeka, Kansas.

In 1874, Singleton, Johnson, and others organized the Edgefield Real Estate and Homestead Association to help African-Americans move to Kansas. Johnson stayed in Topeka to assist the newcomers. Between 1877 and 1879, Singleton traveled throughout the South urging his people to move to the new colonies.

This movement to Kansas and other parts of the west was called the Exodus of 1879. Singleton claimed to be the "whole cause of the Kansas immigration." He printed thousands of posters that stated, "All Colored People That Want to Go to Kansas Can Do So for $5." He felt that his efforts were the reason twenty thousand African-Americans left

Tennessee, Mississippi, Louisiana, and Texas. Singleton became known as the "Father of the Exodus" and "The Moses of the Colored Exodus." His followers were known as "Exodusters." This is his story:

After the war, my race willingly slipped a noose over their necks and knuckled under to a bigger boss than the old one...[By in by] the Fifteenth Amendment came along and...our poor people thought they were going to have Canaan right off. But I knowed better... .

Conditions might be better a hundred year from now when all the present generation is dead and gone, but not afore, sir, not afore, and what's going to be a hundred years from now ain't much account to us in this present...I studied it all out, and it was clear as day to me. I don't know how it came to me; but I suspect it was God's doing. Anyhow I knowed my people couldn't live there...The whites had the lands and

the sense and the blacks had nothing
but their freedom, and it was just like
a dream to them.

Right, emphatically, I tell you
today! I woke up the millions right
through me! The great God of glory
has worked in me. I have had open-
air interviews with the living spirit of
God for my people; and we're going
to leave the South. We're going to
leave it if there ain't an alteration and
signs of a change.

As thousands of African-Americans left the
South, white Southerners became alarmed.
Singleton, along with other movement
leaders, was called before a U.S. Senate
committee in 1880 to explain this great
migration to Kansas.

Well, my people for the want of
land—we needed land for our
children—and their disadvantages
that caused my heart to grieve and
sorrow; pity for my race, sir, that was
coming down, instead of going up—
that caused me to go to work for
them...I am not going to stand

bulldozing and half-pay and all those things...Allow me to say to you that confidence is perished and faded away; they have been lied to every year...My plan is for them to leave the country and learn the South a lesson...We don't want to leave the South, and just as soon as we have confidence in the South, I am going to be an instrument in the hands of God to persuade every man to go back, because that is the best country.

In later years, Singleton decided that African-Americans should leave America and began organizing a migration to Liberia, West Africa. This project failed. Singleton spent the last years of his life in poor health. He died in 1892 in St. Louis, Missouri.

Nia (purpose): To have a plan for the future and to be willing to help others succeed as well.

MARCUS MOSIAH GARVEY'S STORY
You Shall Be Great Again

Marcus Mosiah Garvey was born in St. Ann's Bay, Jamaica, in 1887. Garvey was a large, muscular, dark-skinned man. He was very proud of the fact that he was of pure African blood.

When Garvey was a young man, two events changed the course of his life. He was greatly influenced by an African scholar and newspaper publisher, Duse Mohammed Ali. Garvey met Ali while he was in London. Ali taught Garvey about African history and culture. While in London, Garvey was also introduced to the book *Up from Slavery*, which was written by Booker T. Washington. Washington was president of Tuskeegee Institute, a vocational college for African-Americans. He promoted self-help and industry as the key to uplifting the race.

Upon returning to Jamaica, Garvey began his own self-help organization called the Universal Negro Improvement and Conservation Association and African Communities League (referred to as the U.N.I.A.).

Garvey wrote Washington a letter about the U.N.I.A. and its need for financial support. Washington invited him to come to America. It took years for Garvey to raise the money. Unfortunately, Washington died before Garvey arrived in New York in 1916. However, Garvey was determined to find the funds to support the U.N.I.A. in Jamaica. He began traveling around the United States. Garvey became popular by appealing to working-class African-Americans around the United States and Africans around the world. Through lectures, conventions, and his newspaper, *The Negro World*, Garvey taught his followers to be proud of their African heritage and the beauty of their dark skin. He formed a sharply dressed military-style unit called the African Legion for men and women. Garvey's colorful parades, beautiful uniforms, conventions, speeches, and writings were a source of inspiration to African-Americans, who supported his dreams of a glorious African nation. Garvey taught his followers that the only way African-Americans could reclaim their former greatness was to leave America and return to Africa.

In order to fulfill Garvey's dream of returning to Africa, each member of the U.N.I.A. paid five dollars which went toward purchasing steamships for the Black Star Line. The U.N.I.A. also formed the Negro Factories Corporation in 1919, which gave loans to assist African-Americans who wanted to open stores, factories, and other businesses.

The ships Garvey purchased for the Black

Star Line were not in good repair when purchased, but they were operational. The increasing costs of repairing the ships, and the criticism by other prominent African-American leaders about the way the money for the fleet was handled brought Garvey to the attention of the authorities. In 1922, Garvey was arrested for fraud and imprisoned. Later, it was found that Garvey was innocent of fraud and had been treated unfairly. In 1927, President Calvin Coolidge freed Garvey from prison, but forced him to return to Jamaica.

In 1940, while Garvey was in London, he suffered a severe stroke and died. Garvey never fulfilled his ambition to establish an independent black nation in Africa. However, many African-American businesses began under his leadership. He also created the red, black, and green *bendera* flag that is used as part of the Kwanzaa celebration.

Garvey instilled a new found sense of pride in millions of African-Americans—pride in their heritage, the color of their skin, and their accomplishments. This is what he said:

...We are calling upon the four
hundred million Negroes of the world

to take a decided stand, a determined stand, that we shall occupy a firm position; that position shall be an emancipated race and a free nation of our own. We are determined that we shall have a free country, we are determined that we shall have a flag, we are determined that we shall have a government second to none in the world...

When we come to consider the history of man, was not the Negro a power, was he not great once? Yes, honest students of history can recall the day when Egypt, Ethiopia, and Timbuktu towered in their civilizations, towered above Europe, towered above Asia...Why, then, should we lose hope? Black men, you were once great; you shall be great again.

Kuumba (creativity): To always do as much as we can, in any way we can, in order to leave our community a better and more beautiful place.

JAMES VAN DERZEE'S STORY
A True Picture

James Van DerZee was a self-taught master photographer who was born on June 29, 1886, in Lenox, Massachusetts. At an early age, Van DerZee became a talented still-life artist, pianist, and violinist. He began taking pictures when he was nine years old. In 1900, Van DerZee moved to Harlem in New York City in search of a better job. James and his second wife, Gaynella, opened the Guarantee Photo Studio at 109 West 135th Street in Harlem in 1915. For the next fifty-three years, Van DerZee took photographs of famous and not-so-famous African-Americans. Van DerZee became the official photographer of Marcus Garvey and the Universal Negro Improvement Association (U.N.I.A.). Van DerZee also took photographs of other famous African-Americans such as boxers Harry Wills, Jack Johnson, and Joe Louis; baseball player Satchel Paige; singer Florence Mills and pianist Hazel Scott; and tap dancer Bill "Bojangles" Robinson; as well as thousands of portraits of the everyday lives of African-Americans. Van DerZee became known throughout Harlem as the "Picture-Taking Man."

When Van DerZee was eighty-two, the Metropolitan Museum of Art in New York City "discovered" the thousands of photographs he had taken during his long career. They included a large number of the photos in their

1968 exhibit "Harlem on My Mind." Van DerZee became famous for the artistic quality of his work and his photographs' powerful portrayals of African-American life.

Before the exhibit, many people thought of Harlem as a rundown, crime-ridden slum. Van DerZee's photographs portrayed his Harlem neighborhood in a way that others seldom saw it. His camera captured the day-to-day activities of a proud, lively African-American neighborhood full of hardworking, well-dressed people who loved and cared for their families.

Van DerZee's artistic touch with the camera produced photographs that revealed the common rhythms of Harlem life—love, hate, death, food, family, hope, joy, perseverance, and despair. It is easy to see Van DerZee's pride in his African-American identity and his community. This is his story:

One day, I saw a little advertisement—I think it was in *Youth's Companion*—that said I could get a camera and outfit for selling so many packages of sachet....It must have taken me about two months to sell all of it. There weren't that many people around to sell it to, and when I'd sold some to everyone I could, I had to wait around until they used it up so I could try and sell it again. So I finally sold all the perfume and I sent the money in, and the next day I started running to the post office and the express office looking for this camera and outfit. And finally one day there was a red card in the box in the post office, meaning there was a package too big to go in the mailbox. My blood pressure must have gone up to the bursting point. I grabbed the package and raced back home and went up to my bedroom with it.

I was developing and developing, and one day I saw a scratch across the plate, and I thought that must be the picture. But after I brought it out into the light, I saw that the plate was all black. I couldn't get any results because the camera was too cheap. It was really a box.

Van DerZee was determined to buy a better camera. He worked as a gardener for Mrs. David Dana in Lenox.

> She'd give us twenty-five cents an hour, and I managed to save five dollars. That's how I came to buy my second camera, a box camera. I used to operate it on a stand. It took glass plates, so I did my own developing.

Van DerZee's fifth-grade teacher saw some of his pictures and asked that he take some of his class. It was his first job as a photographer.

> I didn't know people made a living at making pictures in those days. If I had known at that time, I could have made a good living, because I was taking pictures of all the aristocrats; and there was only one other man in Lenox who had a camera. Seeing the interest I had in that type of work, they [my family] were interested, too. After I got the more expensive camera, I began

photographing the family, and they enjoyed seeing the pictures.

Van DerZee's first professional job in New York was as a photographer in a department store.

Some photographer wanted a darkroom man, and I figured I was "dark" enough for the job! The man had a concession in a Goerke's department store. It was a cheap type of work—three pictures for fifty cents, finish while you wait. So, I went and answered this ad, and he said he didn't know. He wanted a man who could photograph, too, and he didn't know if his customers would stand for my photographing or not [because Van DerZee was an African-American and all the customers were white]. So—I figured he knew more about his business than I did—I left. A month or so later, I saw another ad. Not knowing it was the same place, I went back again. This time he decided to try me out. He'd say, "Stand back, I'll make the baby's picture." Bam! The picture would be made. But, I'd take time [with the customers]—you know, sit down and talk to them ahead of time, get their natural expressions and so forth. It was interesting work for me. I got a chance to do some experimenting with lights and different poses. I'd take time to get good pictures of them. Being an artist, I had an artist's instincts. Why, you have an advantage over the average photographer. You can see the picture before it's taken; then it's up to you to get the camera to see it. With the large-size film, I could add a lot with an etching knife and a retouching pencil. I paid attention to the face, I appreciated the face.

Van DerZee became a master at using the multiple-image technique. He printed the negative of one photograph, then reprinted it, adding scenes from another negative.

I guess it was just a matter of not being satisfied with what the camera was doing. I wanted to make the camera take what I thought should be there, too. I wasn't satisfied with just the people's picture. I wanted to see if I could incorporate what they were thinking about, and that [multiple-image technique] was my way of doing it. It wasn't difficult with the proper facilities, and when I had my own studio, I had those facilities.

The "Picture-Taking Man" died on May 15, 1983. He left behind seventy-five thousand classic glass and film negatives and prints of African-Americans in New York. His photographs are valuable not only for their artistic quality, but as a historical document of African-Americans in the early 1900s. Van DerZee's photographs gave people all over the world a different view of the African-American community in Harlem.

Imani (faith): To believe with all our heart in our people, our parents, our teachers, our leaders, and the righteousness and victory of our struggle.

FANNIE LOU HAMER'S STORY
Lighting the Way

Fannie Lou Hamer was the twentieth and last child of Jim and Ella Townsend. Her parents were poor. They worked hard to make a living as farmers. After years of backbreaking work, the family was just beginning to prosper when a jealous white neighbor poisoned all their mules and cows.

Hamer married Perry "Pap" Hamer in 1942 and worked as a cotton picker and timekeeper on the W. D. Marlow plantation in Ruleville, Mississippi. Hamer was a deeply religious woman and was known for the inspiring way she sang. Her theme song was "This Little Light of Mine."

In 1962, Hamer's life changed after attending a special meeting held by the Student Non-Violent Coordinating Committee. The students came to Ruleville to register African-Americans to vote. If African-Americans voted they could elect government officials who would help them better their lives. Voting was a way to gain power.

Many African-Americans who lived in the South were afraid to register. Anyone who registered to vote could lose their jobs, homes, or life. Hamer knew that registering could be dangerous, but she did it anyway. Her decision changed her life. She was beaten, shot at, and left homeless because she wanted to vote. Through it all, Hamer had faith and a determination that her fight for civil rights was a just cause. Hamer felt that working for the rights of African-Americans to be equal in American society was her mission. This is her story:

> He [James Forman of the Student Non-Violent Coordinating Committee] told us...we could vote out people and they talked about how, you know, hateful policemen and how they had been elected and if we had a chance to vote, you know, that we wouldn't allow these people to be in office because we could vote them out. It made so much sense to me.
>
> Until then, I had never heard of no mass meeting and I didn't know that a Negro could register to vote. Bob Moses, Reggie Robinson, Jim Bevel, and James Forman were some of the Student Non-Violent Coordinating Committee workers who ran that meeting. When they asked for those to raise their hands who'd go down to the courthouse the next day, I raised mine. Had it up as high as I could get it. I guess if I'd

had any sense I'd a been a little scared, but what was the point of being scared. The only thing they could do to me was kill me and it seemed like they'd been trying to do that a little bit at a time ever since I could remember.

When we got down there [to the voter's registration office in Indianola, Mississippi] it was so many people down there, you know, and some of them looked like the Beverly Hillbillies...but they wasn't kidding down there; they had on, you know, cowboy hats and they had guns; they had dogs.

It took Hamer three times to pass the complicated literacy test Mississippi required her to take in order to vote. When her employer found out that she had registered to vote, he fired her and made her leave the plantation. Hamer knew that she might be killed for attempting to vote, but she refused to take her name off the voter registration rolls.

Ten days later they fired into Mrs. Tucker's house where I was staying.

They also shot two girls at Mr. Sissel's. That winter was bad.... Pap couldn't get a job nowhere 'cause everybody knew he was my husband. We made it on through, though, and since then I just been trying to work and get our people organized.

I've worked on voter registration here [in Mississippi] ever since I went to that first mass meeting. In 1964, we registered sixty-three thousand black people from Mississippi into the Freedom Democratic Party. We formed our own party because the whites wouldn't even let us register. We decided to challenge the white Mississippi Democratic Party at the National Convention.

Whether you have a PhD, or no D, we're in this bag together. And whether you're from Morehouse or Nohouse, we're still in this bag together. Not to fight to try to liberate ourselves from the men—this is another trick to get us fighting among ourselves—but to work together with the black man, then we will have a better chance to just act as human beings, and to be treated as human beings in our sick society.

You can pray until you faint, but if you don't get up and try to do something, God is not gonna put it in your lap.

This ain't just Mississippi's problem. It's America's problem. If you just stand there and don't lash back, you can find a real human being in a lot of people. I don't never write nobody off. My policy is do unto others as you would have them do unto you. I'd tell the white powers that I ain't trying to take nothing from them. I'm trying to make Mississippi a better place for all of us. And I'd say, "What you don't understand is that as long as you stand with your feet on my neck, you got to stand in a ditch, too. But if you move, I'm coming out. I want to get us both out of the ditch." I'm not saying I don't get angry sometimes. Oh, yes, I do. And when I do, I'll walk up to these folks and say: "Look, now we are going to do something about this. Number one, you can write your dates on the calendar because you ain't getting back in office because we'll vote you out!" And they know I mean it.

I've always believed that one day, even if I didn't live to see it, this country would be different. It would be a place for all people to live, where they could be without the hangings and the lynchings and the killings and the bombings. We are our brother's keeper whether he is black, white, brown, red, or yellow. As the Bible tells us, God made of one blood all nations.

Fannie Lou Hamer died from cancer at the age of sixty. She didn't live to see all of the changes she worked for to make Mississippi and America a better place, but she never lost faith in the cause.

EPILOGUE

African-Americans are like the threads in the *kente* cloth that is woven in West Africa. Each beautiful, silken thread is fragile alone, but when woven together, they make a strong, colorful cloth. The principles of Kwanzaa celebrate the achievements of the individual, the strength of the African-American community, and bring us closer together as a people.

Harambee! Harambee! Harambee! Harambee! Harambee! Harambee! Harambee!

GLOSSARY

Swahili is one of the most popular languages in Africa. Although the dialect is different from country to country, more than forty-five million people in eastern Africa, and in most of Kenya, Tanzania, Rwanda, Burundi, Zambia, and Somalia speak a form of Swahili.

The proper name for Swahili is Kiswahili. The prefix *ki* is a definition of the actual language as opposed to the people who speak the language. For example, a person speaking Swahili would refer to the language spoken by the Ganda people as Kiganda.

There are only twenty-four letters in the Swahili alphabet. There is no sound for Q or X in the language. Swahili vowels are pronounced as follows:

a is pronounced like the a in far
e is pronounced like the a in say
i is pronounced like the ee in see
o is pronounced like oe in toe
u is pronounced like the oo in coo

Swahili consonants are pronounced the same way they are in English. G has a hard sound such as in give. R is like the Spanish R and is made by rolling the tongue. Place the accent on the next-to-last syllable in most Swahili words, unless otherwise indicated:

Bendera (ben-de-ra): National Black Liberation Flag. The bendera is black, red, and green and is similar to one that was first made popular by Marcus Garvey. Black is for the color of the people, red is for the struggle that is carried on by Africans and African-Americans for a better life, and green is for the future that will result from the struggle.

Habari gani (ha-ba-ri ga-ni): A Swahili term that means, "What's the news?"

Harambee (ha-ram-bee): A Swahili word that means, "Let's all pull together!"

Imani (i-ma-ni): One of the seven principles of Kwanzaa. It means faith in Swahili.

Karamu (ka-ra-mu): This is the feast that is held on the evening of December 31st.

Kikombe cha umoja (ki-kom-be cha u-mo-ja): The unity cup. This cup is passed in honor of the family ancestors, and as a sign of unity.

Kinara (ki-na-ra): A candle holder. A symbol of our African ancestors, the root from which the family evolved.

Kuchunguza tena na kutoa ahadi tena (ku-chu-ngu-za te-na na ku-toa a-ha-di te-na): The speech that helps the audience to remember the things Kwanzaa teaches.

Kujichagulia (ku-ji-cha-gu-lia): One of the seven principles of Kwanzaa. It means self-determination in Swahili.

Kukumbuka (ku-kum-bu-ka): Short speech by a member of the audience on the meaning of Kwanzaa.

Kukaribisha (ku-kar-i-bi-sha): The welcoming ceremony that is held at the beginning of the *karamu* feast.

Kushangilia (ku-shan-gi-lia): To rejoice.

Kutoa majina (ku-toa ma-ji-na): The calling of the names of the family ancestors, as well as African-American heroes and heroines.

Kuumba (ku-um-ba): One of the seven principles of Kwanzaa. It means creativity in Swahili.

Kwanza (kwan-za): The term means "first" in Swahili.

Kwanzaa (kwan-za): A cultural holiday created in 1966 by Dr. Maulana Karenga.

Libation statement: The speech that is made before passing the communal unity cup *(kikombe cha umoja)*.

Mazao (ma-za-o): Crops. A bowl of fruit and vegetables is placed on a mat, the *mkeka*, to represent the rewards of working together.

Mishumaa saba (mi-shu-ma-a sa-ba): The seven candles. Three red, one black in the center, and three green, are placed in the *kinara*. Each candle represents one of the *Nguzo Saba* (seven principles) of Kwanzaa.

Mkeka (m-ke-ka): Mat. The *mkeka* is a symbol for unity and represents a firm foundation to build on. All the symbols of Kwanzaa are placed on the *mkeka*.

Muhindi (mu-hin-di): The ears of corn that are used to represent children during Kwanzaa.

Nguzo Saba (n-gu-zo sa-ba): A term that means "seven principles" in Swahili. The *Nguzo Saba* is the guide for daily living. This guide is studied during Kwanzaa, to be practiced throughout the year.

Nia (ni-a): One of the seven principles of Kwanzaa. It means purpose in Swahili.

Ngoma (n-go-ma): The drum performance given during the *karamu* feast.

Swahili (swa-hi-li): A nontribal African language used in many parts of Africa.

Tamshi la tambiko (tam-shi la tam-bi-ko): The libation speech that is read before passing the unity cup.

Tamshi la tutaonana (tam-shi la tu-ta-o-na-na): The farewell speech that is given at the end of the *karamu* feast.

Ujamaa (u-ja-ma): One of the seven principles of Kwanzaa. It means cooperative economics in Swahili.

Ujima (u-ji-ma): One of the seven principles of Kwanzaa. It means collective work and responsibility in Swahili.

Umoja (u-mo-ja): One of the seven principles of Kwanzaa. It means unity in Swahili.

Zawadi (za-wa-di): The gifts given during Kwanzaa as a reward for the commitments made and kept during the holiday.